A Heart for God

Inspiration
for
Dads

A Heart for God

Inspiration
for
Dads

Adapted from *Bible Wisdom for Fathers*
by Gary Wilde

Compiled by Mark R. Littleton

ChariotVICTOR
PUBLISHING
A DIVISION OF COOK COMMUNICATIONS

Victor Books is an imprint of ChariotVictor Publishing, a division of Cook
Communications, Colorado Springs, Colorado 80918
Cook Communications, Paris, Ontario
Kingsway Communications, Eastbourne, England

2 3 4 5 6 7 8 9 10 Printing/Year 01 00 99 98 97

Introduction

Oh, the difficulties of being a father in today's world. Not only is he expected to bring home the bacon, but also love his wife, maintain the home, discipline the children, lead the family in devotions and spiritual living, and grow his own spiritual life so that he can truly become a man of God.

Such fathers often feel daunted.

Herein is help.

This little book contains many powerful, well-known and little-known Scriptures that will impel a father on toward his goals with freedom and hope in his stride. Each page features a small chunk of Scripture meant to speak to a specific need, perhaps a need that the Spirit of God will have orchestrated in his life for that day.

You fathers may want to memorize some of these verses too so you don't have to carry around the book in your pocket because the verse will be in your heart.

Drink in, father, and remember that God is with you. And I will do—I Myself will grant—whatever you may ask in My name [presenting all I AM] so that the Father may be glorified and extolled in [through] the Son. [Yes] I will grant—will do for you—whatever you shall ask in My name [presenting all I AM]. If you [really] love Me, you will keep [obey] My commands. And I will ask the Father, and He will give you another Comforter (Counselor, Helper, Intercessor, Advocate, Strengthener and Standby) that He may remain with you forever, the Spirit of Truth, whom the world cannot receive (welcome, take to its heart), because it does not see Him, nor know and recognize Him. But you know and recognize Him, for He lives with you [constantly] and will be in you. I will not leave you orphans—comfortless, desolate, bereaved, forlorn, helpless—I will come [back] to you (John 14:13-18, AMP).

*N*o man is alone:

I will not leave you as orphans; I will come to you (John 14:18, NIV).

God's love for all:

A father of the fatherless, and a judge of the widows, is God in his holy habitation (Ps. 68:5).

2

*H*ow to respond to God:

He shall cry to Me, "You are my Father, my God, and the rock of my salvation!" (Ps. 89:26, AMP)

*G*od's outlook on His children:

"And I will be a father to you, And you shall be sons and daughters to Me," says the Lord Almighty (2 Cor. 6:18, NASB).

A *prayer to the Great Father:*

Our Father which art in heaven, hallowed be thy name. Thy kingdom come. Thy will be done in earth, as it is in heaven. Give us this day our daily bread. And forgive us our debts, as we forgive our debtors. And lead us not into temptation, but deliver us from evil: for thine is the kingdom, and the power, and the glory for ever. Amen (Matt. 6:9-13).

5

*G*od provides:

And I will do —I Myself will grant — whatever you may ask in My name [presenting all I AM] so that the father may be glorified and extolled in [through] the Son. [Yes] I will grant — will do for you — whatever you shall ask in My name [presenting all I AM]. If you [really] love Me, you will keep [obey] My commands. And I will ask the Father, and He will give you another Comforter (Counselor, Helper, Intercessor, Advocate, Strenghthener and Standby) that He may remain with you forever, the Spirit of Truth, whom the world cannot receive (welcome, take to its heart), because it does not see Him, nor know and recognize Him. But you know and recognize Him, for He lives with you [constantly] and will be in you. I will not leave you orphans — comfortless, desolate, bereaved, forlorn, helpless — I will come [back] to you (John 4:13-18, AMP).

6

*H*ow God sees children:

See that you do not despise one of these little ones, for I say to you, that their angels in heaven continually behold the face of My Father who is in heaven (Matt. 18:10, NASB).

*G*od's concern to reach His people in all places and times:

What do you think? If a man has a hundred sheep and one of them has gone astray, does he not leave the ninety-nine on the mountains and go and search for the one that is straying? And if it turns out that he finds it, truly I say to you, he rejoices over it more than over the ninety-nine which have not gone astray. Thus it is not the will of your Father who is in heaven that one of these little ones perish (Matt. 18:12-14, NASB).

*G*od will *always provide:*

Every good and perfect gift is from above, coming down from the Father of the heavenly lights, who does not change like shifting shadows (James 1:17, NIV).

9

*T*he Father has shown Himself:

Philip said to Him, "Lord, show us the Father, and it is sufficient for us." Jesus said to him, "Have I been with you so long, and yet you have not known Me, Philip? He who has seen Me has seen the Father; so how can you say, 'Show us the Father'? Do you not believe that I am in the Father and the Father is in Me? The words that I speak to you I do not speak on My own authority; but the Father who dwells in Me does the works. Believe Me that I am in the Father and the Father in Me, or else believe Me for the sake of the works themselves" (John 14:8-11, NKJV).

*G*od's love:

How great is the love the Father has lavished on us, that we should be called children of God! And that is what we are! The reason the world does not know us is that it did not know him (1 John 3:1, NIV).

What we have in Christ:

Praise be to the God and Father of our Lord Jesus Christ, who has blessed us in the heavenly realms with every spiritual blessing in Christ. For he chose us in him before the creation of the world to be holy and blameless in his sight. In love he predestined us to be adopted as his sons through Jesus Christ, in accordance with his pleasure and will—to the praise of his glorious grace, which he has freely given us in the One he loves. In him we have redemption through his blood, the forgiveness of sins, in accordance with the riches of God's grace that he lavished on us with all wisdom and understanding. And he made known to us the mystery of his will according to his good pleasure, which he purposed in Christ, to be put into effect when the times will have reached their fulfillment—to bring all things in heaven and on earth together under one head, even Christ (Eph. 1:3-10, NIV).

*G*od molds us:

Yet, O Lord, You are our Father; we are the clay, and You are the

potter and we all are the work of Your hand (Isa. 64:8, AMP).

We *have an internal Father, who speaks daily:*

And because ye are sons, God hath sent forth the Spirit of his Son into your hearts, crying, "Abba, Father!" Wherefore thou art no more a servant, but a son; and if a son, then an heir of God through Christ (Gal. 4:6-7).

God watches:

He raises up the needy out of distress, and makes their families like flocks. The upright see it and are glad; and all wickedness stops its mouth. Let all who are wise give heed to these things; and consider the steadfast love of the Lord (Ps. 107:41-43, NRSV).

15

Nothing can separate us from our Father in heaven:

No, in all these things we are more than conquerors through him who loved us. For I am convinced that neither death nor life, neither angels nor demons, neither the present nor the future, nor any powers, neither height nor depth, nor anything else in all creation, will be able to separate us from the love of God that is in Christ Jesus our Lord (Rom. 8:37-39, NIV).

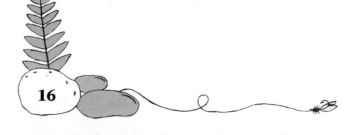

God watches over all, from the greatest to the lowest:

Are not two little sparrows sold for a penny? And yet not one of them will fall to the ground without your Father's leave and notice (Matt. 10:29, AMP).

17

*W*e are children of the eternal Father:

See how great a love the Father has bestowed upon us, that we should be called children of God (1 John 3:1, NASB).

*G*od's acceptance:

[God] accepts men from every nation who fear him and do what is right (Acts 10:35, NIV).

19

*G*od chose each of us:

Blessed be the God and Father of our Lord Jesus Christ, who hath blessed us with all spiritual blessings in heavenly places in Christ: According as he hath chosen us in him before the foundation of the world, that we should be holy and without blame before him in love: having predestinated us unto the adoption of Jesus Christ to himself, according to the good pleasure of his will, to the praise of the glory of his grace, wherein he hath made us accepted in the beloved (Eph. 1:3-6).

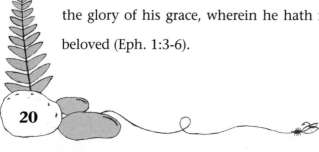

*W*e are heirs:

For as many as are led by the Spirit of God, these are sons of God.
For you did not receive the spirit of bondage again to fear, but you
received the Spirit of adoption by whom we cry out, "Abba, Father."
The Spirit Himself bears witness with our spirit that we are children
of God, and if children, then heirs—heirs of God and joint heirs
with Christ, if indeed we suffer with Him that we may also be glorified together (Rom. 8:14-17, NKJV).

*H*ow to address our Father in heaven:

And because you are children, God has sent the Spirit of his Son into our hearts, crying, "Abba! Father!" So you are no longer a slave but a child, and if a child then also an heir through God (Gal. 4:6-7, NRSV).

*N*o Christian need fear others:

I, even I, am He who comforts you. Who are you that you are afraid
of a man who dies, and of the son of man who is made like grass?
(Isa. 51:12, NASB)

*G*od comforts us:

As one whom his mother comforts, so will I comfort you (Isa. 66:13, AMP).

God comforts us so we can comfort others:

Praise be to the God and Father of our Lord Jesus Christ, the Father of compassion and the God of all comfort, who comforts us in all our troubles, so that we can comfort those in any trouble with the comfort we ourselves have received from God (2 Cor. 1:3-4, NIV).

God leads:

He shall feed his flock like a shepherd; he shall gather the lambs with his arm, and carry them in his bosom, and shall gently lead those that are with young (Isa. 40:11).

*G*od sanctifies:

Say to the Israelites, Truly you shall keep My sabbaths, for it is a sign between Me and you throughout your generations, that you may know that I, the Lord, sanctify you (set you apart for Myself) (Ex. 31:13, AMP).

*G*od heals:

And He said, "If you will give earnest heed to the voice of the Lord your God, and do what is right in His sight, and give ear to His commandments, and keep all His statutes, I will put none of the diseases on you which I have put on the Egyptians; for I, the Lord, am your healer" (Ex. 15:26, NASB).

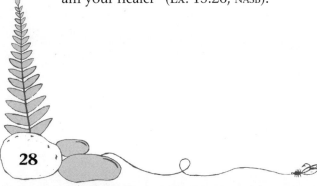

*G*od wins the battle:

And Joshua defeated Amalek and his people with the sword. Then the Lord said to Moses, "Write this as a reminder in a book and recite it in the hearing of Joshua: I will utterly blot out the remembers of Amalek from under heaven." And Moses built an altar and called it, The Lord is my banner (Ex. 17:13-15, NRSV).

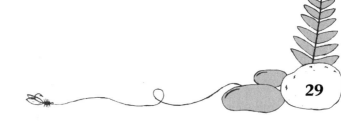

God gives peace:

So Gideon built an altar there to the Lord, and called it The-Lord-Shalom (Jud. 6:24, NKJV).

*G*od provides:

So Abraham called that place "The Lord will provide." And to this day it is said, "On the mountain of the Lord it will be provided" (Gen. 22:14, NIV).

God will be in our midst forever:

The circumference of the city shall be eighteen thousand cubits. And the name of the city from that time on shall be, The Lord is there (Ezek. 48:35, NRSV).

*G*od is all-powerful:

Thus saith the Lord, thy redeemer, and he that formed thee from the womb, I am the Lord that maketh all things; that stretcheth forth the heavens alone; that spreadeth abroad the earth by itself (Isa. 44:24).

33

God is perfect and eternal:

And God said to Moses, I AM WHO I AM and WHAT I AM, and I WILL BE WHAT I WILL BE; and He said, You shall say this to the Israelites, I AM has sent me to you (Ex. 3:14, AMP).

*J*esus *is the fullness of the Godhead:*

For in Him all the fulness of Deity dwells in bodily form, and in Him you have been made complete, and He is the head over all rule and authority (Col. 2:9-10, NASB).

*G*od protects:

God is my strong fortress; He guides the blameless in his way and sets him free (2 Sam. 22:33, AMP).

*H*as anyone ever called you a fool? Then remember:

God has chosen the foolish things of the world to shame the wise, and God has chosen the weak things of the world to shame the things which are strong (1 Cor. 1:27, NASB).

*A*re you acting the fool? Then think on this:

Are you so foolish? After beginning with the Spirit, are you now trying to attain your goal by human effort? (Gal. 3:3, NIV)

*O*ur light is Christ:

Then spake Jesus again unto them, saying, "I am the light of the world: he that followeth me shall not walk in darkness, but shall have the light of life" (John 8:12).

*H*ow we serve God:

We must work the works of Him who sent Me, as long as it is day; night is coming, when no man can work. While I am in the world, I am the light of the world (John 9:4-5, NASB).

Jesus therefore said to them again, "Truly, truly, I say to you, I am the door of the sheep. All who came before Me are thieves and robbers; but the sheep did not hear them. I am the door; if anyone enters through Me, he shall be saved, and shall go in and out, and find pasture. The thief comes only to steal, and kill, and destroy; I came that they might have life, and might have it abundantly" (John 10:7-10, NASB).

*H*e tends his flock like a shepherd:

He gathers the lambs in his arms and carries them close to his heart;

he gently leads those that have young (Isa. 40:11, NIV).

*G*od's reward to those who serve Him:

And when the chief Shepherd shall appear, ye shall receive a crown of glory that fadeth not away (1 Peter 5:4).

*G*od's work for His people:

Just as You sent Me into the world, I have sent them into the world (John 17:18, AMP).

*G*od's commandment:

A new commandment I give to you, that you love one another, even as I have loved you, that you also love one another (John 13:34, NASB).

*T*he depth of God's love in Christ to His people:

Be imitators of God, therefore, as dearly loved children and live a life of love, just as Christ loved us and gave himself up for us as a fragrant offering and sacrifice to God (Eph. 5:2, NIV).

45

***C**hrist's prayer for His children:*

But I have prayed for you, Simon, that your faith may not fail. And when you have turned back, strengthen your brothers (Luke 22:32, NIV).

*G*od's assurance to those who fear:

Wherefore he is able also to save them to the uttermost that come unto God by him, seeing he ever liveth to make intercession for them (Heb. 7:25).

A right attitude:

Let this mind be in you which was also in Christ Jesus, who, being in the form of God, did not consider it robbery to be equal with God, but made Himself of no reputation, taking the form of a servant, and coming in the likeness of men. And being found in appearance as a man, He humbled Himself and became obedient to the point of death, even the death of the cross (Phil. 2:5-8, NKJV).

*A*ssurance for those who sin:

My little children, I am writing these things to you so that you may not sin. But if anyone does sin, we have an advocate with the Father, Jesus Christ the righteous (1 John 2:1, NRSV).

*C*hrist understands us:

Therefore, holy brethren, partakers of a heavenly calling, consider Jesus, the Apostle and High Priest of our confession. He was faithful to Him who appointed Him, as Moses also was in His house (Heb. 2:17-18, NASB).

*C*hrist beckons to us:

For we do not have a high priest who is unable to sympathize with our weaknesses, but we have one who has been tempted in every way—yet was without sin. Let us then approach the throne of grace with confidence, so that we may receive mercy and find grace to help us in our time of need (Heb. 4:15-16, NIV).

Christ has always been there, and always will be there for people of faith:

In the beginning [before all time] was the Word [Christ], and the Word was with God, and the Word was God Himself. . . And the Word [Christ] became flesh [human, incarnate], and tabernacled—fixed His tent of flesh, lived awhile—among us; and we [actually] saw His glory—His honor, His majesty, such glory as an only begotten son receives from his father, full of grace (favor, loving kindness) and truth (John 1:1, 14, AMP).

*W*e call God our Father, even as Jesus did:

Jesus said to them, "My Father is always at his work to this very day, and I, too, am working." For this reason the Jews tried all the harder to kill him; not only was he breaking the Sabbath, but he was even calling God his own Father, making himself equal with God (John 5:17-18, NIV).

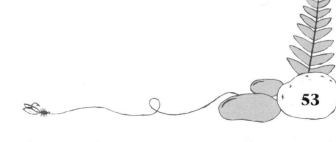

*W*e are "in" Christ Jesus:

But by His doing you are in Christ Jesus, who became to us wisdom from God, and righteousness, and sanctification, and redemption (1 Cor. 1:30, NASB).

*W*e see the Father in Christ:

Jesus cried and said, "He that believeth on me, believeth not on me, but on him that sent me. And he that seeth me seeth him that sent me" (John 12:44-45).

*C*hrist's sacrifice for people:

For he hath made him to be sin for us, who knew no sin; that we might be made the righteousness of God in him (2 Cor. 5:21).

*O*ur source of hope:

And He Himself bore our sins in His body on the cross, that we might die to sin and live to righteousness; for by His wounds you were healed. For you were continually straying like sheep, but now you have returned to the Shepherd and Guardian of your souls (1 Peter 2:24-25, NASB).

*T*he heavenly house-builder:

For every house is builded by some man; but he that built all things is God (Heb. 3:4).

*H*ow we build our house:

Through skillful and godly Wisdom is a house [a life, a home, a family] built, and by understanding it is established [on a sound and good foundation] (Prov. 24:3, AMP).

*O*ur *foundation:*

He will be the sure foundation for your times, a rich store of salvation and wisdom and knowledge; the fear of the Lord is the key to this treasure (Isa. 33:6, NIV).

*O*ur greatest gift to God:

Present yourselves as building stones for the construction of a sanctuary vibrant with life, in which you'll serve as holy priests offering Christ-approved lives up to God (1 Peter 2:5, TM).

A warning:

For what will it profit them if they gain the whole world but forfeit their life? Or what will they give in return for their souls? (Matt. 16:36, NRSV)

*H*ow to love God:

He who loves father or mother more than Me is not worthy of Me. And he who loves son or daughter more than Me is not worthy of Me. And he who does not take his cross and follow after Me is not worthy of Me. He who finds his life will lose it, and he who loses his life for My sake will find it (Matt. 10:37-39, NKJV).

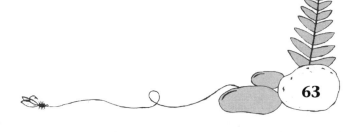

A foolish man:

And he told them this parable: "The ground of a certain rich man produced a good crop. He thought to himself, 'What shall I do? I have no place to store my crops.'

"Then he said, 'This is what I'll do. I will tear down my barns and build bigger ones, and there I will store all my grain and my goods. And I'll say to myself, "You have plenty of good things laid up for many years. Take life easy; eat, drink and be merry."'

"But God said to him, 'You fool! This very night your life will be demanded from you. Then who will get what you have prepared for yourself?' This is how it will be with anyone who stores up things for himself but is not rich toward God" (Luke 12:16-21, NIV).

*A*void legalism:

If you have died with Christ to the elementary principles of the world, why, as if you were living in the world, do you submit yourself to decrees, such as, "Do not handle, do not taste, do not touch"? (Col. 2:20-21, NASB)

***G**od sees all we are and do:*

For the ways of man are before the eyes of the Lord, and He ponders all his paths (Prov. 5:21, NKJV).

A *right outlook:*

I will meditate on all your work, and muse on your mighty deeds
(Ps. 77:12, NRSV).

What to think about:

Finally, brethren, whatever is true, whatever is honorable, whatever is right, whatever is pure, whatever is lovely, whatever is of good repute, if there is any excellence and anything worthy of praise, let your mind dwell on these things (Phil. 4:8, NASB).

*A*n invitation:

Come to Me, all who are weary and heavy-laden, and I will give you rest. Take My yoke upon you, and learn from Me, for I am gentle and humble in heart; and you shall find rest for your souls. For My yoke is easy, and My load is light (Matt. 11:28-30, NASB).

God is our source of strength:

The Lord is my strength and my shield; my heart trusts in him, and I am helped. My heart leaps for joy and I will give thanks to him in song. The Lord is the strength of his people, a fortress of salvation for his anointed one (Ps. 28:7-8, NIV).

*T*he value of a person in God's eyes:

Are not two sparrows sold for a penny? Yet not one of them will fall to the ground apart from the will of your Father. And even the very hairs of your head are all numbered (Matt. 10:29-30, NIV).

God's promise:

But unto you that fear my name shall the Sun of righteousness arise with healing in his wings; and ye shall go forth, and grow up as calves of the stall (Mal. 4:2).

A promise of reward everlasting:

Delight yourself also in the Lord, and He will give you the desires and secret petitions of your heart (Ps. 37:4, AMP).

The test of a man's love for Christ:

He who has My commandments and keeps them, he it is who loves Me; and he who loves Me shall be loved by My Father, and I will love him, and will disclose Myself to him (John 14:21, NASB).

*G*od's protection:

So you think that I cannot appeal to my Father and he will at once send me more than twelve legions of angels? (Matt. 26:53, NRSV)

*R*each out to the needy:

"For I was hungry and you gave me something to eat, I was thirsty and you gave me something to drink, I was a stranger and you invited me in, I needed clothes and you clothed me, I was sick and you looked after me, I was in prison and you came to visit me." Then the righteous will answer him, "Lord, when did we see you hungry and feed you, or thirsty and give you something to drink? When did we see you a stranger and invite you in, or needing clothes and clothe you? When did we see you sick or in prison and go visit you?" The King will reply, "I tell you the truth, whatever you did for one of the least of these brothers of mine, you did for me" (Matt. 25:35–40, NIV).

*H*elp when it's needed:

But whoever has this world's goods, and sees his brother in need, and shuts up his heart from him, how does the love of God abide in him? (1 John 3:17, NKJV)

We have been visited by angels:

Do not neglect to show hospitality to strangers, for by this some have entertained angels without knowing it (Heb. 13:2, NASB).

*T*he Christian's ultimate resource:

And be not drunk with wine, wherein is excess; but be filled with the Spirit; speaking to yourselves in psalms and hymns and spiritual songs, singing and making melody in your heart to the Lord; giving thanks always for all things unto God and the Father in the name of our Lord Jesus Christ; submitting yourselves to one another in the fear of God (Eph. 5:18-21).

A caution:

But godliness actually is a means of great gain, when accompanied by contentment. For we have brought nothing into the world, so we cannot take anything out of it either. And if we have food and covering, with these we shall be content. But those who want to get rich fall into temptation and a snare and many foolish and harmful desires which plunge men into ruin and destruction. For the love of money is a root of all sorts of evil, and some by longing for it have wandered away from the faith, and pierced themselves with many a pang (1 Tim. 6:6-10, NASB).

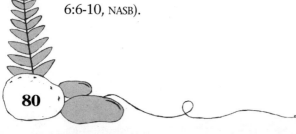

*T*he basic principle of marriage:

Marriage should be honored by all, and the marriage bed kept pure, for God will judge the adulterer and all the sexually immoral (Heb. 13:3-4, NIV).

The admonition to husbands:

Husbands, love your wives, just as Christ loved the church and gave himself up for her, in order to make her holy by cleansing her with the washing of water by the word, so as to present the church to himself in splendor, without a spot or wrinkle or anything of the kind —yes, so that she may be holy and without blemish. In the same way, husband should love their wives as they do their own bodies. He who loves his wife loves himself. For no one ever hates his own body, but he nourishes and tenderly cares for it, just as Christ does for the church, because we are members of his body. For this reason a man will leave his father and mother and be joined to his wife, and the two will become one flesh. This is a great mystery and I am applying it to Christ and the church. Each of you, however, should love his wife as himself, and a wife should respect her husband (Eph. 5:22-33, NRSV).

*H*ow a husband treats his wife before his children:

Likewise you husbands, dwell with them with understanding, giving honor to the wife, as to the weaker vessel, and as being heirs together of the grace of life, that your prayers may not be hindered (1 Peter 3:7, NKJV).

On adultery:

You have heard that it was said, "Do not commit adultery." But I tell you that anyone who looks at a woman lustfully has already committed adultery with her in his heart (Matt. 5:27-28, NIV).

An example of one who failed:

When Esau heard the words of his father, he cried with an exceedingly great and bitter cry, and said to his father, "Bless me, even me also, O my father!" But he said, "Your brother came with deceit and has taken away your blessing." And Esau said, "Is he not rightly named Jacob? For he has supplanted me these two times. He took away my birthright, and now look, he has taken away my blessing!" And he said, "Have you not reserved a blessing for me?" (Gen. 27:34-36, NKJV)

A *blessing for us all:*

Now may the God of hope fill you with all joy and peace in believing, that you may abound in hope by the power of the Holy Spirit (Rom. 15:13, NASB).

A prayer for us all:

Now may the God of peace, who brought back from the dead our Lord Jesus, the great shepherd of the sheep, by the blood of the eternal covenant, make you complete in everything good so that you may do his will, working among us that which is pleasing in his sight, through Jesus Christ, to whom be the glory forever and ever. Amen (Heb. 13:20-21, NRSV).

A *promise:*

And my God will meet all your needs according to his glorious riches in Christ Jesus (Phil. 4:19, NIV).

*O*ur source of power and guidance:

And I will ask the Father, and he will give you another Counselor to be with you forever—the Spirit of truth. The world cannot accept him, because it neither sees him nor knows him. But you know him, for he lives with you and will be in you…. But the Counselor, the Holy Spirit, whom the Father will send in my name, will teach you all things and will remind you of everything I have said to you. Peace I leave with you; my peace I give you. I do not give to you as the world gives. Do not let your hearts be troubled and do not be afraid (John 14:16-17, 26-27, NIV).

A verse to memorize and store in our hearts:

Trust in the Lord with all thine heart; and lean not unto thine own understanding. In all thy ways acknowledge him, and he shall direct thy paths (Prov. 3:5-6).

*P*aul's goal for God's people:

For this reason, I bow my knees before the Father, from whom every family in heaven and on earth derives its name, that He would grant you, according to the riches of His glory, to be strengthened with power through His Spirit in the inner man; so that Christ may dwell in your hearts through faith; and that you, being rooted and grounded in love, may be able to comprehend with all the saints what is the breadth and length and height and depth, and to know the love of Christ which surpasses knowledge, that you may be filled up to all the fulness of God (Eph. 3:14-19, NASB).

*R*elating to the world:

Do not be conformed to this world—this age, fashioned after and adapted to its external, superficial customs. But be transformed (changed) by the [entire] renewal of your mind— by its new ideals and its new attitude—so that you may prove [for yourselves] what is the good and acceptable and perfect will of God, even the thing which is good and acceptable and perfect [in His sight for you] (Rom. 12:2, AMP).

*O*n discipline:

No, I beat my body and make it my slave so that after I have preached to others, I myself will not be disqualified for the prize (1 Cor. 9:27, NIV).

How the Father feels about His people:

Like as a father pitieth his children, so the Lord pitieth them that fear him (Ps. 103:13).

94

*T*he priority of faith:

It is impossible to please God apart from faith. And why? Because anyone who wants to approach God must believe both that he exists and that he cares enough to respond to those who seek him (Heb. 11:6, TM).

*G*od's assurance of training and guidance for all of us:

I will instruct you and teach you in the way you should go; I will counsel you with my eye upon you (Ps. 32:8, NRSV).

*H*ow *we regard our nation:*

If My people who are called by My name will humble themselves, and pray and seek My face, and turn from their wicked ways, then I will hear from heaven, and will forgive their sin and heal their land (2 Chron. 7:14, NKJV).

On enemies:

But I say to you, love your enemies, and pray for those who persecute you in order that you may be sons of your Father who is in heaven; for He causes His sun to rise on the evil and the good, and sends rain on the righteous and the unrighteous (Matt. 5:44-45, NASB).

*O*n *work:*

You must have accurate and honest weights and measures, so that you may live long in the land the Lord your God is giving you. For the Lord your God detests anyone who does these things, anyone who deals dishonestly (Deut. 25:15-16, NIV).

*O*n honor:

Whoever will humble himself therefore, and becomes [trusting, lowly, loving, forgiving] as this little child, is greatest in the kingdom of heaven (Matt. 18:4, AMP).

On the heart:

And let the peace of God rule in your hearts, to the which also ye are called in one body; and be ye thankful (Col. 3:15).

*O*n *our children:*

Train children in the right way, and when old, they will not stray (Prov. 22:6, NRSV).

*O*n God's word:

And these words which I command you today shall be in your heart; you shall teach them diligently to your children, and shall talk of them when you sit in your house, when you walk by the way, when you lie down, and when you rise up. You shall bind them as a sign on your hand, and they shall be as frontlets between your eyes. You shall write them on the doorposts of your house and on your gates (Deut. 6:6-9, NKJV).

On *the family:*

Do not hold back discipline from the child, although you beat him with the rod, he will not die (Prov. 23:13, NASB).

On our parents:

Honor your father and your mother, as the Lord your God has commanded you, so that you may live long and that it may go well with you in the land the Lord your God is giving you (Deut. 5:16, NIV).

On training:

My son, keep your father's [God-given] commandment, and forsake not the law of [God] your mother [taught you] (Prov. 6:20, AMP).

*O*n temptation:

No temptation has overtaken you but such as is common to man; and God is faithful, who will not allow you to be tempted beyond what you are able, but with the temptation will provide the way of escape also, that you may be able to endure it (1 Cor. 10:13, NASB).

***G**od's assurance to those in the midst of temptation:*

But the Lord is faithful, and He will strengthen and protect you from the evil one (2 Thes. 3:3, NASB).

*O*n the fear of the Lord:

He who listens to a life-giving rebuke will be at home among the wise. He who ignores discipline despises himself, but whoever heeds correction gains understanding. The fear of the Lord teaches a man wisdom, and humility comes before honor (Prov. 15:31-33, NIV).

*O*n *pride:*

A man's pride will bring him low, but he who is of a humble spirit shall obtain honor (Prov. 29:23, AMP).

On commitment:

Do you not know that those who run in a race all run, but one receives the prize? Run in such a way that you may obtain it. And everyone who competes for the prize is temperate in all things. Now they do it to obtain a perishable crown, but we for an imperishable crown. Therefore I run thus: not with uncertainty. Thus I fight: not as one who bears the air. But I discipline my body and bring it into subjection, lest, when I have preached to others, I myself should become disqualified (1 Cor. 9:24-27, NKJV).

***O**n good works:*

So let us not grow weary in doing what is right, for we will reap at harvest time (Gal. 6:9, NRSV).

*O*n destiny:

I again saw under the sun that the race is not to swift, and the battle is not to the warriors, and neither is bread to the wise, nor wealth to the discerning, nor favor to men of ability; for time and chance overtake them all. Moreover, man does not know his time: like fish caught in a treacherous net, and birds trapped in a snare, so the sons of men are ensnared at an evil time when it suddenly falls on them (Ecc. 9:11-12, NASB).

113

*G*od's promise to His people in all places and times:

Be strong and of a good courage, fear not, nor be afraid of them; for the Lord thy God, he it is that doth go with thee; he will not fail thee, nor forsake thee (Deut. 31:6).

*O*n fear:

For God did not give us a spirit of timidity, but a spirit of power, of love and of self-discipline (2 Tim. 1:7, NIV).

On our burdens:

Cast your burden on the Lord, and He shall sustain you; He shall never permit the righteous to be moved (Ps. 55:22, NKJV).

*O*n *worship:*

Let them praise His name in chorus and choir and with the [single or group] dance, let them sing praises to Him with the tambourine and lyre! (Ps. 149:3, AMP)

*H*ave no fear:

There is no fear in love. But perfect love drives out fear, because fear has to do with punishment. The man who fears is not made perfect in love (1 John 4:18, NIV).